FRACTURED:

A Miracle Along the LA Marathon

Helene "Gloria" Morris

Copyright © 2024 Helene Morris

All rights reserved

ISBN: 9798333606549
Imprint: Independently published

Cover Photo: David Morris
Cover Design: Helene Morris

This book is dedicated to Eliza Fletcher. Though I never met you, I continue to feel and experience the profound ripple effect of your life.

The God of all grace, who called you to his eternal glory in Christ, will Himself restore, establish, strengthen, and support you after you have suffered a little while.

1 PETER 5:10

CONTENTS

Title Page
Copyright
Dedication
Epigraph
FRACTURED
Chapter 1: The Start Line   1
Chapter 2: Marathon on My Mind   16
Chapter 3: Marathon Weekend   30
Chapter 4: My Race   39
Chapter 5: After The Marathon   63
References and Inspiration   71
About The Author   75

FRACTURED

CHAPTER 1:
THE START LINE

My plan for the 2024 Los Angeles Marathon downward spiraled from me running all 26.2 miles in the high 10-minute per mile range, to just making it across the start line. Yes, the start line. The finish line, I figured, was already a lost cause. At that point, I had renegotiated my marathon dream so many times that I arrived at Dodger Stadium with this iteration: I was going to cross the start line, walk for a couple of minutes, have my cheerleader husband take a few photos, and then head home. Maybe we would even make it back in time for a nice lunch. A chicken Caesar salad in lieu of a finisher medal. Little did I know, my life was about to change.

We arrived at Dodger Stadium just as the race was starting.

I was uncharacteristically calm since being late is such a trigger and stressor for me. Runners are corralled based on their previous marathon finish times. Corral A, for example, held the elite runners with a sub 3:15:59 marathon time, or an average pace of less than seven minutes and 30 seconds per mile, for all of 26.2 miles. The seeded corrals go all the way to E, which is a sub 5:00:59 marathon, or a pace less then 11:30 per mile.

And then there is the open corral for everyone else, people like me who had never run a marathon or folks who had completed a marathon, but at a slower pace: basically, anything over five hours and one minute, an 11:31-minute per mile average pace and higher. The idea is to start the race in waves from fastest to slowest. Professional runners, the very elite, start before Corral A. It makes for a real race, grouping runners based on their speed. This system keeps slower runners from blocking faster runners, creates a safer environment, and saves people from being bumped into, or even worse, falling down and being trampled on. Plus, it's fair. Everyone wears a bib with a chip, so the clock is personalized, beginning when each individual runner crosses the start line.

One month earlier, I thought that my 2024 Los Angeles Marathon results would for sure qualify me for Corral E placement the following year, in 2025. Afterall, I finished the Long Beach Half Marathon in October 2022 at 2:18:43, a 10:35 per mile pace. Double that time, and I would be at 4:37:26 for my marathon. I could do this thing in less than five hours. I ran my best 5K (3.1 miles), at an 8:58 per mile average pace in July 2023. Me, the 44-year-old woman who had somehow bypassed middle and high school P.E. and decided to run the first mile of her life at the ripe age of 41.

It's amazing how that happened. My first mile at age 41. I had generational bondage about running spoken over my life at such a young age. In my earliest memory, I am a kindergartener, and my P.E. teacher has arranged a special parent teacher conference for my mom to watch me run. I remember running around the small grassy patch behind our school lunch tables while my mom and P.E. teacher stood side by side in serious conversation. Then, we left, in a speed walking huff toward the car as my mom curtly told my P.E. teacher, "That's how *I* run." My mom could not run. Her mom could not run. I could not run. That was my mom, the protector.

The funny thing is, I became a teacher, an elementary school principal, and later a district level administrator. Reframing this memory through my eyes as an educator brought so many questions to the surface. Decades later, my mom and I would have a conversation that went something like this:

"Mom, in kindergarten, when my P.E. teacher asked you to watch me run, was it impromptu? Like, did she catch you in the parking lot at drop-off or pickup and ask if you had a few minutes because she was concerned about my running?"

"No," my mom replied, matter of fact. "It was a conference."

"When you say conference…?"

"She called me and set it up in advance so that I could watch you run, because she thought that you ran funny. But I just told her, that's how I run." When I replay this conversation in my mind, I hear it in my mom's voice, fired up and dripping with irritation. The audacity of my P.E. teacher!

At the same time, I can feel for my P.E. teacher, who was well intentioned, trying to help her five-year-old student. In a career that has spanned more than two decades, I cannot recall a single time, when a P.E. teacher I have worked with or supervised has called a parent to come to school to watch their child run. My poor mom! Her child's running was so very concerning that it warranted both a conference and a demonstration. Some might take what my P.E. teacher did as criticism, but to me it now seems like the act of a caring adult. Nevertheless, even good intentions have consequences, and for me it would be more than 35 years until I changed my thinking and believed that I could run.

In July of 2020, I started walking occasionally. Like so many people, I needed fresh air, a break from the confines of the pandemic, and an escape from the clinical depression and anxiety that I wrestled with in my mind. I asked my friend Natasha to teach me about the local trails that she often walked, and then I discovered the wealth of trails just across the street at our local regional park. On February 8, 2021, I was out for a roundtrip 3.52-mile solo walk at this very park. I had the day off from work, and I was a few weeks away from defending my dissertation at USC. I had more editing to do, and I remember thinking that I wanted to get home faster. I wondered if, after months of walking, could I run a single mile? I set my phone app to test myself, and I ran one mile at an 11:25 pace. I finished the month of February running six miles and walking 32.02 miles. Three years later, in February 2024, I finished the month having run 140.51 miles.

Running is an interesting sport because most of the non-runners I have met say they "hate running." I do not hear that consistently spoken about any other sport. Fill a room of 200 random people. How many will say they "hate basketball" or any other sport as opposed to running? There's something about running that seems to cause an instant and precise reaction in people… maybe it stems back to the general population's negative experiences with having to "run the mile" in school. I thought I hated running too. H.A.T.E.D. Plus I could not do it, or so I thought. I believed the lie.

Then there's the irony. In order to love running, a person has to do something they hate over and over again until there's a shift that happens and the hate turns into love or some other positive emotion. Running is a multiplication sport. For some people, like me, it takes some time to work up to that first 5K, the first 3.1 miles, but once a person can run for about three miles or 30 minutes continuously, the multiplication begins, and it becomes easier to add on miles from there. Five months after I ran my first mile, I ran my first 5K race. Then, a little more than a year after that first mile (in May of 2022), I ran my first half marathon.

My whole way of thinking shifted. I read Christopher McDougall's *Born to Run*, and I went from believing I was destined to never run, to cherishing running as part of the very fiber of my being. McDougall's book talks about different running theories like barefoot running. When I went into a running store – A Snail's Pace – to be fitted for my first pair of "real" running shoes, I told the sales person that I wanted a shoe that mimicked barefoot running. The salesperson later brought his trainee out to help me, or more or less observe me, his eccentric customer. That's when myself awareness kicked in – I was *that* customer – so in the end, I walked away with some decent (and pricy) running shoes and realized that I would not be running barefoot.

Running changed my whole world because, first, it changed what I believe, then how I think, and finally my outward reality. I have studied and learned so much about childhood trauma, and the Adverse Childhood Experiences (or ACES as they are called). I have given multiple presentations on this topic, been promoted to oversee Social-Emotional Learning (SEL) for an entire school district, and become an absolute fan of Dr. Nadine Burke Harris' *The Deepest Well*, which is a book I presented about and highlighted to the school board where I work. Through all of this, I have come to learn that I did not face a great deal of childhood trauma. There are some situations where I look back now and realize that I could have been abused, and I credit my mom for protecting me.

My trauma came as an adult. For years and years, my husband and I tried to get pregnant. I still remember the day I found out I was pregnant – via IVF – as one of the happiest days of my life. Then, when I went to the first ultrasound to hear my baby's heartbeat, it was silent. I was 35-years-old. I remember having to go back to work that night because I was the school principal, and it was parent information night for sixth grade science camp. I felt like a zombie, like the shell of a person I once was. My baby's heartbeat never came, but the report back about her did: she was a healthy chromosomally normal baby girl. I named her Hadley. When I had IVF, two embryos were implanted into me, and I later had a dream, that the second embryo was a little boy named Jackson. My hope rests in the fact that I truly believe that I will get to meet my children one day. But at that time, my heart bled and howled. I was honestly afraid that I would lose my mind if I ever lost another child. I did not believe I could bear that pain again… it seemed like too much of a risk.

I was at the end of myself. Or so I thought. Two years later, on October 5, 2016, my dad – my dad with the high ACE score of eight of 10 childhood traumas – took his life, hanging himself from the rafters of the garage at my parents' home. That took me to the end of myself. My whole life I had heard that I was "just like my dad." When my mom admired something about me like my persistence, focus, or different way of thinking, she would lovingly remark that I was just like my dad. And, when I did something that was not so admirable, like showing a lack of patience or being too competitive, she would also remark, "You're just like your dad."

If I was "just like my dad," and my dad had committed suicide, then who did that make me? Statistically, it made me a first degree relative – parent, child, or sibling – of someone who had committed suicide, and therefore four to six times more likely to commit suicide.

I was so afraid of the stigma of mental health, that I told no one at my work. When people would ask how my dad died, I would tell my half-truth in a quick exasperated mumble, "My dad had a stroke, and it was downhill from there." I did not reveal that my dad had tried to kill himself with pills a few months before his actual death by suicide and that he was accessing multiple mental health resources. Nor did I reveal what my mom later shared... when my dad was in his early 20's, before my parents were married, he also made an attempt to take his life.

Two years passed, and I held it all inside. Because I thought I was good at that, the pretending, using my perfectionist tendencies as a coping mechanism. Then one day, sweating, planking, and praying hard, I had this vision that I would share my story. I was in charge of a full day conference for our junior high/middle school teachers in the school district where I work. I selected myself as the keynote speaker, and I shared the story of my dad, "Duane's story", as I called it, to over 200 people who knew me. My secret was out, and I was loved and embraced for my bravery.

But I did not leave suicide behind at that conference. The spirit of suicide haunted me with a vengeance. Over and over and over and over again. There was not a day when I did not think about suicide. Not. A. Single. Day.

After my dad died, my alcohol consumption increased. My food consumption increased. The insomnia became more than I could bear. I wanted a companion in my misery, so it is not surprising that I encouraged my husband, David, to come along with me for the ride, the dangerous downward spiraling path of self-destruction.

But even then, it was too much to bear. It wasn't until Ramina, my best friend from childhood, told me that I seemed depressed, with such kindness and acceptance, that I finally went to my doctor for help. After screening and assessing me, my doctor confirmed what my friend suspected: I had every marker for clinical depression.

Then, I did what I really needed to do all along: I cried out to God, and my prayers were answered. I was finally ready and willing to change. I asked David, "Aren't you sick of it?" The drinking. He was. I had gone to so many alter calls at church, laying down drinking, knowing full well, that I intended to go and have a bottomless Sunday champagne brunch afterwards. I was such a hypocrite. But by the grace of God, I was finally ready to lay alcohol down.

I quit drinking the only way I knew how to do anything: by reading a book, Allen Carr's *Quit Drinking Without Willpower*. I read the book out loud to my husband. I had my last glass of wine on December 29, 2017, and I have not touched alcohol since. It has come with time, but I have no desire for alcohol whatsoever, and I know I will never drink again. I make no negotiations with myself. No compromises. I will never be a recreational drinker. I will never give alcohol the position or power it had in my life or my husband's life. I am so grateful for this gift, this miracle.

There's a funny thing about drinking though. It's a coping mechanism. I was not prepared for the emotions I would have to face when alcohol was no longer there to cover up my feelings and numb my senses. A few weeks after my husband David and I quit drinking, our church entered into a 21 day fast. This seemed like the perfect opportunity to pray and be mindful about what we were and were not eating. The fast was ultimately the first motivator to change our diet. It would mean saying goodbye to our nightly "snack", more like a "second dinner", that consisted of a big plate filled with cheese, olives, salami, nuts, hummus, pita chips, and general charcuterie board fare. We would eat this meal in bed, watching television, while downing full glasses of red wine. I was so ready for change. With alcohol, went the extra food consumption, and then the weight. My husband and I lost 100 pounds together (70 for him, and 30 for me), and we have kept the weight off.

At work, I was a rockstar, holding myself to high standards of excellence. At the encouragement of a colleague, I applied and was accepted into the doctoral program at USC. Physically, I looked healthier. Time after time, I would run into people I had not seen for a few months, and they would tell me I looked "great" or sometimes even gasp and say they hardly recognized me. I was no longer ruled by alcohol, sugar, unhealthy foods, or excessive eating. But I was dominated by my powerful emotions.

Growing up, my dad used to tell, "Damnit girl! You can't cry every time something doesn't go your way!" I wanted to please my dad, so I learned not to cry. I learned to manage my vulnerability. I most certainly never cried at work. Then, when alcohol went away, and the stress of work and the doctoral program were ever increasing, I just stuffed my emotions inside all day long and started crying in my safe space at home. Sometimes for hours at a time. I would go into a mental pit consumed by thoughts of suicide. My poor husband had to live through this, and he was not equipped to handle it.

But running. Running was equipped to handle my emotions. By June of 2021, four months after I ran my first mile, I was running every day, a couple of miles each morning before work. These morning runs felt like a covering over me, and because of them, I could handle whatever the day brought. I did not know it at the time, but a strong body of research exists about the power that running and cardiovascular exercise has over anxiety and depression. *Running is My Therapy*, by Scott Douglas, is an excellent resource to learn more about this very compelling research.

At the time, I knew nothing about this research, only how I was feeling, or more to the point, how I was not feeling. I started getting up at 4:00 a.m. daily, reading my Bible, journaling, reading other texts, and then taking off for a run a little before 5:30 a.m. I ran in the mornings when winter came, a California winter with temperatures in the 40s and sometimes low 30s that felt cold to my body. I ran in the dark with a headlamp on. I also ran alone in the park. I carried a pepper spray, a knife David made me put in my fanny pack, a noise maker, and courage. I never listened to music because I wanted to be completely aware of my surroundings. I would often see a man out there named Gary, walking his dog, Buck. I had introduced myself as Helene, which is a tricky name, and somehow, he started calling me Olivia. I felt safe with Gary and Buck out there. I know it seems crazy, running in a park, by myself, alone in the dark, but for me, it was a risk I was willing to take for the sake of my mental health. And I needed the outdoors, the fresh air, the experience of nature. I could not go back into the pit of crying, to suicide taking up real estate in my mind. So, I ran by myself in the park for a little more than a year.

On September 2, 2022, all of that changed when Eliza Fletcher, a 34-year-old Memphis Tennessee teacher, was abducted and killed while out for her 4am morning run. This was when my husband David decided that he was going to go running with me every day. By this point, I was running a 5K a day. David would go out and run part of the way. Looking back on my journals, I have September 21, 2022 as the day David became a runner and hit the three-mile mark for the first time. Like me, he did something he hated over and over again, until he fell in love with it. I also felt very loved, that my husband would do something like this for me and my safety… both my physical and mental safety. We would later learn in a church marriage group that a man's greatest need is respect, and a woman's greatest need is safety.

In October, I completed my second half marathon, and a few weeks later, on October 29, 2022, David and I participated in the OC United 5K Pumpkin Run. As I neared the finish line, I felt pain in the knee area of my right leg that would continue long after the race was over. An MRI would ultimately reveal a tibial fracture in my right knee area.

The fracture was a stress fracture or what is called an overuse fracture. I ran almost 1,000 miles in 2022, before the fracture. I ran so much I cracked my bones. I was particularly vulnerable because I had high calcium disease, also known as Hypercalcemia. Basically, I had a benign tumor or adenoma growing on my parathyroid (located behind the thyroid). The growth was blocking my body from absorbing calcium, which is why I had calcium running through my bloodstream in excess. On July 5, 2018, I successfully had surgery to remove one of my four parathyroid glands, and I was healed. But the aftereffects stayed. In my late 30s, I began getting bone density scans, and I was diagnosed with osteopenia.

Now, I was fractured and out of the running game. That was a "come to Jesus" moment, literally. Had I placed running above God? Even worse, had I made running my God? It seemed to me that I had decided my mental health problems were too big for God, but not too big for running. I realized that I had stopped praying hard, long, and daily prayers. My prayer life was like my right knee: fractured.

I rehabbed with the Lord. I kept with my 4am morning routine, planking, praying, and doing physical therapy in lieu of running. My physical therapist gave me hope and said, "I believe you will run again." He gave me a research based running rehabilitation program out of the University of Delaware's Physical Therapy Clinic.

On February 23, 2023, a rainy Saturday morning, David and I purchased a used treadmill from a kind elderly gentleman on Facebook Marketplace. It was bitter sweet. We went to the man's home and garage. As I was testing the treadmill, the man shared that he had bought the treadmill for his wife who has Parkinson's Disease. He assembled it for her, and she tried the treadmill one time before they came to the conclusion that it would not work for her. My heart ached for this family, and I thought of them often as I worked my way back to running, alternating walking and running, until I could consecutively jog three miles about two months later.

CHAPTER 2:

MARATHON ON MY MIND

I was back in the game. David and I were running again in the mornings. And I was prayer running, talking to God the entire time. A surprising side effect was that I learned to talk and run. Before my injury, I never seemed to have enough wind in my lungs to talk and run. Now, it was as it should be: running at a comfortable pace and carrying on a conversation with my Lord and Savior.

I was more grateful than ever to be running again. I had some setbacks. I did not run for the entire month of August 2023 when I got Planter Fasciitis in my left foot. I felt a little sorry for myself, a bit like the biblical Job. But I went to physical therapy and learned one exercise in particular that had a dramatic effect on my problem. I iced my foot every morning and every evening. And then I made the decision: I was going to run with pain. And I did. Eventually, by keeping consistent with prayer, icing, and physical therapy exercises, the pain in my foot became almost nonexistent.

It was time to start dreaming again, and I had marathon on my mind. What was I waiting for? "Today," I told myself, "is the youngest you will ever be." I had faced and overcome so many obstacles. If my dream was to run a marathon, there was no sense in waiting, because as I had learned with my health, anything can happen.

Like most people, I like to find evidence to support my beliefs and dreams. I was therefore drawn to Hal Elrod's *The Miracle Morning* which spells out the life transforming practice of waking up early and having a morning routine. What I love most about reading, is that one book often points to another, and it's usually a book I would never find on my own. In this case, that book was *The Non-Runner's Marathon Trainer* by David A. Whitsett, Forrest A. Dolgener, and Tanjala Mabon Kole. These three authors wrote this book based on their collective experience teaching and/or participating in a marathon class at the University of Northern Iowa. Their program is research based, and the authors say that anyone who follows this program will finish the marathon.

That is the goal, to finish the marathon. At least the first time. My vision of running miles in the 10-minute range and completing a marathon in less than five hours, all needed to be laid down. As the book explains, "If you do exactly what we tell you to do, you WILL finish this marathon. If that (finishing) is the goal you have set, you WILL have a success experience. However, if you set a target time and then miss it, even by a few minutes, you will have converted what could have been one of the greatest success experiences of your life into a failure! Please don't do that to yourself. The goal should be to complete the marathon, regardless of the time it takes," (pg. 4). Little did I know how true those words would ring for me. Finish the marathon, no matter how long it takes.

I set my sights on the Los Angeles, or LA Marathon, as it is often called. Over time, I learned that running without people is not ideal. I needed to make friends in the running world. Sometimes, I was so overly zealous, that when I found a person who ran, I would geek out and talk about running to the point where I missed the social cues that it was time to let the person escape from their conversation with me. But that is how I learned that locally, the LA Marathon is the best first marathon. From the incredible course, to the legacy, to the cheering fans, and encouragement mile by mile, it would be the ideal first marathon.

I put my beautiful Type A mind to work, and mapped out and scheduled every single run of my 16-week training program leading up to the March 17, 2024 LA Marathon on St. Patrick's Day. The authors of *The Non-Runner's Marathon Trainer* describe their training program as modest compared to other programs. For example, some programs require five days of running; this program only requires four days. Some programs work the longest run up to 20 miles; this program's longest runs are 18 miles. Nevertheless, 18 miles seemed pretty daunting to me.

The program is structured with three weekday runs and one long Saturday run. Six of the Saturday runs were in excess of a 13.1-mile half marathon: one 14-mile run; three 16-mile runs; and two 18-mile runs. The program peeks at Week 13 with 36 miles, broken down as two five-mile runs, an eight-mile run, and an 18-mile run. I completed every run, and all six of the half-marathon-plus runs: a total of 356.4 miles. Then, halfway through Week 14 (of 16), I felt that oh-so-familiar pain in my right knee.

I was so close. In the program I was following, the weekly running miles drop dramatically the last few weeks before the marathon to allow the body to rebuild glycogen stores. I was a mere 38 miles away from completing my training program. I had run from my home in Anaheim to the Honda Center three times and to Angel Stadium two times. Eventually, every Saturday morning became the longest run of my life. An 18-mile run was certainly a challenge for me, so I ran slowly and steadily, around a 12-minute per mile pace, for over three hours at a time.

The mornings before work were also grueling. For a slow runner like me, running eight miles before work meant getting up at 3:45 a.m. and running for 90 minutes, the majority of the time in the dark, in a headlamp, relishing those last few miles, when the sun would rise so perfectly and gloriously, and I would become one with the dawn.

And David was with me, during all of the morning runs, many of the Saturday runs, including two of the 16 milers. He is a big fan of the Ducks, so it was so exciting, to actually run to the Honda Center with him, where the Ducks play. During Week 5, I told David, "You know, you have completed five weeks of marathon training." He started to get excited, and he seriously considered running the marathon, until his hip and knee pain became too great.

David and I joined a running group through our church. The group was very small and helped at the beginning of my training, until there was no one at my pace or distance, and I eventually had to go at it alone. I had to relearn how to run such long distances alone. My training program did not recommend training with music, and I never felt safe doing so. Then a few things happened: David added me to our Apple Music family account; the long runs were, well, long; and I discovered motivational speech songs.

It surprises me that motivational speech songs are not talked about more in our culture. I found them by deliberately searching through Apple Music for motivational and inspiring music. They are literally a short speech, sort of like a rap, set to music or a beat. These songs – mostly I listened to Fearless Motivation and Billy Alsbrooks – fired me up during my (fully lit, well populated, and safe) Saturday morning runs!

The Bible talks about taking "every thought captive," (2 Cor 10:5). Controlling my thoughts meant controlling my emotions. These songs, played over and over again, rewrote the narrative of my mind. I learned to fight back, to be a champion, to get comfortable in the presence of pain, to be a beast, to stay in the game, and to not give up on my dream.

And what was my dream? To finish the LA Marathon. For me, the LA Marathon had become more than an achievement. I believed that when I crossed the finish line, I would forever lay down every ounce of depression, every suicidal ideation, that I would step into my true destiny, and activate the next step in the divine purposes for my life. It's a lot of pressure and responsibility for one marathon. I challenged myself. Was this narcissistic or grandiose thinking? Were my thoughts irrational? Maybe. But it was a risk I was willing to take because I was so supercharged. I wanted the marathon as much as I wanted any goal I had ever pursued. I believed that when I crossed the finish line, I would supernaturally receive, from heaven, a **new name** like Simon Peter or the Apostle Saul who became Paul. Even David had a hard time with that one, "I'm not sure about this new name, Helene." At the heart of it, what I wanted was real transformation, a ground breaking monumental life achievement where I would be forever changed into the next best version of myself. And having a name that was easier to pronounce would not be so bad, right?

To add to all of the running, I decided that I wanted to try my hand at body building. I came across Instagramer Denise Kirtley @fiftyfitnessjourney. I could relate to her story because of my own metamorphosis via diet and exercise. I saw that weight lifting held a promise of fitness and strength beyond running. True to form, I decided to learn about weightlifting by reading a book. I read *Thinner Leaner Stronger* by Michael Matthews. I brought David on board. We cleaned out our garage, bought a weight rack cage, a standard Olympic barbell, and began adding to our equipment. The barbell weighs 45 pounds, and I cried when I realized I could not even do one bench press with it. That was in October 2023. Now I can bench press the barbell, squat the barbell, and deadlift the barbell, with weights/plates added. Strength training was a recommended part of my running program, so everything seemed to be aligning for me.

Still, I had my doubts. I did not know if I could complete

the marathon. I had the Planter Fasciitis in my left foot under control, just as the tendinitis in my right foot was increasing in pain. I became a super stretcher. My left knee, the one that had not been fractured, had been causing me problems with the long runs. Allegedly, it had the beginning stages of arthritis. I say allegedly because I rejected that medical diagnosis. These were the vulnerable spots in my mind, where doubt, fear, and confusion crept in.

I had this big important goal, but I could not visualize it in my mind. I had February 12, 2024 off from work for President's Day. I did my eight-mile run that morning and then in the afternoon went into our garage for a workout. I remember the exact moment that God gave me the vision. My AirPods were in and Andra Day's "Rise Up" was blasting into my ears as my foot was pressed firmly against the wall of our laundry room doing Planter Fasciitis physical therapy exercises. The vison came so clearly in my mind's eye. I saw myself crossing the finish line of the LA Marathon. In that moment, tears of gratitude spilled from my eyes as I looked toward heaven, filled with such peace and joy. I saw it. I would finish; my dream would come true, and with it, the blessing. This vision came two days after I had completed a 21-day period of corporate prayer and fasting with our church, Influence Church in Anaheim. The vision alone seemed like a miracle.

And then, it all started to slowly unravel. Two weeks later, after another eight-mile run, I noticed a pain in my right knee. The knee I had fractured. The knee that an x-ray showed was healed and strengthened from a fracture. The knee that my doctor told me would not be at risk for another fracture. That knee. I waited two days and did my next five-mile morning run on February 29th. Normally, I run my last mile a little faster than the other miles in my run. That day, I could not; in fact, I ran it slower and with a mild limp. No, no, no. This could not be happening. Not again. Not when I was so close.

I took the next morning off from running, and David and I tried running later that day after work. The pain set in immediately. Pain, that despite all of those motivational speech songs imprinted into my brain, I did not want to push through because I did not want to make it worse. I made the difficult decision to take a week off from my training and running program.

I also entered into another time of prayer and fasting for the two weeks leading up to the marathon. I began a study of Esther, for "such a time as this." My fast consisted of a protein shake in the morning and dinner after work, along with two full days of no food. Normally when I fast, I do not try or consider losing weight. That is not the goal of fasting. This time, however, I wanted weight loss as an added benefit. I wanted to reduce the inflammation in my body, and I knew that even dropping a few pounds could take strain off of my knee.

Eight days later, on Saturday, March 9, 2024, David and I set out again. As we began our run, my arms shot up into the air in victory. The pain was so mild. I was back, and I was so happy. This victory, however, was fleeting, and by the time I finished the second mile, I was in misery. The pain was great as was my concern to not risk further injuring myself. David completed the five-mile run, and I walked the rest of the way home, only traversing 3.89 miles. After our run, David and I went to watch a basketball tournament for my work. There, my thoughtful co-workers were asking me about my morning run and my upcoming marathon. The last thing I wanted to do was speak life into an injury that I did not want to accept or believe for myself. So, I held it all inside and shared only good things. Just like I did when my dad died.

I went to urgent care later that afternoon, and the physician's assistant I saw was a triathlete. She did not dismiss my dream. She took x-rays, gave me a steroid shot and prescription, and made an expedited referral to orthopedics. Three days later, I was at the orthopedic surgeon's office.

"You're back," he said.

My x-rays were good. A healed fracture. Unfortunately, as I had learned almost a year and a half ago, stress fractures do not typically show up on x-rays. An MRI is needed to diagnose a fracture, which can take a couple of months to get approved and scheduled. He would order another MRI, but I needed an answer *now* because the LA Marathon was five days away.

Based on a physical examination, all signs pointed to another stress fracture and the crushing of a dream.

"Could I run the LA Marathon?" I asked.

"No," my doctor replied.

"Could I walk the LA Marathon?"

"No."

"No? Well, why not?"

Because I could fall. And if I fell, I could ruin my knee and have to have a metal plate put in, and a bunch of other things that sounded like womp-womp. It did not matter because my pain was too great to walk or run the LA Marathon.

"But, could I further injure myself?"

"Yes," he said, firmly and absolutely.

I wasn't entirely convinced.

I was at a crossroads, and I did not know what to do. I was questioning everything about myself. I had seen that vision of me crossing the finish line, clear as day, and I felt it. Not an emotion, but something deeper. Like looking back on a photograph or a memory of something that already existed. I had experienced this type of assuredness before. In times when I wanted something so much, when my desire was burning inside of me, I would see that goal accomplished in the future, and all I needed to do was step into it, to just keep moving forward on the path that I was on, and that future would come to me. Our church pastors have shared so many times that we have to "say what we want to see" and "call those things that are not as though they are." Some people call this manifestation. I believed it was my God given destiny.

The human mind is funny, ridiculous at times. Here I had this vision that I believed was from my BIG God of the entire universe, that pointed to the divine purposes for my life, and in my brokenness (literally) and humanity, I started to question it. I started to weigh the costs. That prompted feelings of guilt. I had paid over $200 to register in the LA Marathon and another $150 for Start Line Hospitality, so I could wait for the race to begin in heated tents with food, places to sit, and restrooms that did not have lines a mile deep. It was all nonrefundable. Then, there were the costs we had not yet incurred like parking and our stay at The Biltmore, a historic hotel in the heart of downtown Los Angeles. We could have driven up from East Anaheim to Dodger Stadium the morning of the marathon, but it seemed too hectic with crowds of 25,000+ people expected, the 7:00 a.m. start time, and the even earlier expected arrival time. Plus, all participants were required to pick up their race bibs the day before, on Saturday March 16th, at the Lifestyle Expo held at Dodger Stadium. Technically, I could get my bib the day of the race because I had purchased Start Line Hospitality, but I heard trying to ride the shuttles without a bib could cause delays. Then, there was my mom, who was driving up from San Diego to housesit and watch our three dogs. My spring break was conveniently scheduled the week following the race, and my mom and I were planning to spend time together while I rested and recovered. I had not told my mom about my injury. I had not told anyone except my husband.

David, true to form – the guy who proofread every paper I wrote in my doctoral program including my dissertation – was as supportive as ever. He thought we should go to the Lifestyle Expo and stay at the Biltmore Hotel. The morning of the race was up to me, he said.

I was still fasting and praying. I knew the only way I was going to cross the finish line and run – or even walk – the race was through a true miracle from God. And how could I ever receive my miracle if I did not exercise some measure of faith? How could I expect a miraculous healing if I was not even willing to show up for the race to receive the miracle. I had to *go to* the race.

My mind kept going to the well-known Old Testament story of Daniel in the den of lions. Lions. Plural. Daniel was in that den all night, and there was no escaping: the den was sealed with a stone. The king wanted Daniel to live, and so he refused entertainment, fasted, and could not sleep. In the early morning, the king hurried out to the lions' den and called out in anguish, "Daniel, servant of the living God! Was your God, whom you serve so faithfully, able to rescue you from the Lions?" Daniel answered, "Long live the king! My God sent his angel to shut the lions' mouths so that they would not hurt me, for I have been found innocent in his sight, and I have not wronged you, Your Majesty," (Daniel 6:20-22, NLT).

Delivered, not devoured. What a creative solution to just shut the mouths of the lions. Why did I not think of that? Maybe because I am not God. In fact, when it comes to my faith and obedience, I am not even close to being like Daniel. But I serve the same God. And if God could shut the mouths of lions for Daniel, he could do that for me. But first, I would have to walk into the lions' den. If I wanted to step into the miracle, I had to willingly step into the lions' den and trust God. I made up my mind: I would show up to the LA Marathon, and I would, at the very least, cross the start line and begin the race.

CHAPTER 3:
MARATHON WEEKEND

My mom arrived at my house the afternoon of Friday, March 15th. I made sure I was as cheerful as possible when I got home from work after another epically exhausting and stressful day. I could walk without limping, and I was careful to make sure my mom did not see any indication of my pain or injury. My mom had her own troubles: a torn meniscus that had been healing for several months along with undiagnosed pain in her other knee. I figured I would tell her everything after we got home from the race. Although, somehow, her mother's intuition knew. As she hugged me goodbye on Saturday morning so we could head out to the Lifestyle Expo, she sounded protective and a bit sad for me, "I just pray that you finish this race," she said, hugging me tightly and pressing her lips into my freshly washed hair.

My mom was not my only supporter. While I had shared my LA Marathon dream with a fairly small circle, those who did know me, reached out with words of encouragement. The most interesting being my best friend Ramina, from childhood: the one who boldly and aptly told me years ago that I seemed depressed. Ramina sent me a picture of a candle and a rock and said she was burning the candle for me. We grew up across the street from one another, and she was so close to my family that she called my parents mom and dad. She explained that my dad gave her the rock in 2002, when my parents moved from Anaheim to Jamul, a rural part of East County San Diego. There, my parents bought 10 acres of land – Ramina's rock came from this land – and built the house that my dad would one day take his life in. But, seeing an image of this special rock that Ramina had kept and treasured for over two decades… how could I possibly tell her that short of a miracle I was not running (or likely completing) the marathon? So, I basically told her what I told everyone who reached out to me, "thank you."

David and I walked around the Lifestyle Expo at Dodger

Stadium, took lots of pictures, and I mostly tried not to worry that I was walking too much. And then I worried about worrying because those were limiting beliefs. We ate an early dinner and went back to our hotel room to rest because we would be getting up at 3:30 a.m. the next morning for the marathon. Our room had this unique feature that would turn out to be a nightmare. The door to our room, 808, was also labeled 810. Both of these rooms shared one common door that led to a tiny square of an entry and then each room had its own individual door.

As it so happened, the woman in room 810 was celebrating her 35th birthday. Loudly. Exuberantly. Her friends started arriving, slamming the shared door back and forth, in and out of their room. They were laughing, squealing with delight, and it sounded like they were having the time of their lives. Fortunately, they were going out later – or so I thought because I could hear their animated talking through the walls – but after two hours, later still had not come. We called the front desk, and there were no rooms we could move to; the hotel was fully booked. Did they want us to send up security? No. Why, I wondered, was I the decision maker here? I'm a manager at work, not at this hotel. And, if it was my decision, I was not about to ruin this woman's 35th birthday.

I tried to relax, get comfortable, and ready for bed. Our room was on the smaller side, but it had a rather large walk-in closet with an overhead light that turned on with the tug of a long metal chain. As I was unpacking my suitcase and taking out my pajamas, I noticed a small black object on the floor. I picked it up, turned it over, and read the simple inscription on what I realized was a soft magnet: "do more." All lower case. Do more (period). Do more what? I was like an insect with 1,000 antennas, hypersensitive to the smallest of messages. Was I supposed to "do more" at the race? Go further? Was God nudging me forward?

I stretched out on the bed and started reading through the LA Marathon Race Program that we picked up earlier in the day. Oh, my aching and longing heart as I read through the amazing "Course Tourism" section and all of the sights to be seen and experienced. Chinatown was at mile two of the marathon. Could I make it to mile two? Doubtful. I had walked so much at the Expo earlier that day that I was slightly limping as I moved about our hotel room. I most definitely would not make it to Silver Lake at mile seven to see the Hollywood sign.

Meanwhile, the birthday party next door, was exuding party vibes and volume. We called the front desk again. My teetotaler mind was pulling all the stops. Maybe hotel management could invite the ladies to have some complimentary birthday drinks in the bar? Get them out of the room and downstairs to continue their celebration in another location. The hotel staff informed us that the rooms were for sleeping, and parties were not allowed.

We once again declined their offer to send security up (although they sent them anyway, and I knew because we could hear *everything*).

Nevertheless, I knew that I was only intending to cross the start line of the LA Marathon. Therefore, I was able to be more relaxed about our less-than-ideal sleeping situation. But David was bothered, and it takes a lot to bother David.

"The enemy is really trying to attack us," David said. By enemy he meant the devil, which I know to some people makes us sound like crazy Christians. But spiritual warfare is real. The enemy comes to steal, kill, and destroy. Literally. Through listening to motivational speech songs, I thought more and more about who I was at war with, about who was my opponent, my enemy. Every culture has an enemy; in modern psychology we grapple with our ego. In *The Four Agreements*, author Don Miguel Ruiz explains how the ancient Toltec referred to the enemy as the "parasite" who lives in our minds. We are at war with ourselves. And whoever the enemy is, I learned that I need to look him in the eye and fight back, so that he knows he's not ready for me.

Then, I started to get excited. If it was true – all of these attacks, injuries, roadblocks, obstacles, recent noise developments – and the enemy was really attacking me, then somehow, in my small life, me crossing the start line of the LA Marathon had real significance. It would have been so much easier to say to David,

"We got my marathon shirt, lots of great pictures with me and my bib at the Expo, and we are not going to sleep well in our room, so let's forget about getting up early and have a nice leisurely morning and try to enjoy the hotel amenities until checkout time." That would have been easy. But I'm all about doing hard things. And if the enemy was in fact trying to keep me from crossing the start line of the LA Marathon, then he just played his hand wrong by creating so many obstacles that he revealed the value of what I was about to do.

Just before bed David asked me, "So what are you going to wear tomorrow?"

"Wear? What do you mean?"

"Like, are you going to get in full gear?"

"Yes, I am going to put on my running clothes, my belt, my Gatorade. If I am expecting a miracle, I need to show up. Ready."

"So, are you just going to see what happens?"

"See what happens? No. I am going to cross the start line, take some pictures, and we are going to go home. Then I will write about it: why I chose to cross the start line of the LA Marathon. Tell me you knew this, right? You didn't think I was just going to play it by ear. You knew this when we came here, right?"

"Yes," he assured me, "it's just you were mentioning Chinatown earlier, and so I didn't know."

"I can't walk two miles!" I exclaimed.

"Ok, I'm sorry," and my sweet husband threw up his hands in exasperation, covered his face, shook his head and said, "I'm sorry, I don't know what to say to you."

Supercharged. Your husband is not your enemy. The enemy is your enemy. I mentally repeated this over and over again.

And yet, the enemy still had me confused. I was saying and doing things that were in opposition of each other. I was going to put on my full gear and expect a miracle. And yet, I was just going to cross the start line. Which one was it? Did I really have faith that God was big enough for both my problem and for my dream. Was I scared to do this thing? The literal marathon before me?

◆ ◆ ◆

Sleep came, and then just as quickly, the 3:30 a.m. alarm buzzing on my Garmin watch and also on my phone. This day that I had dreamed about, fasted about, prayed about, and put so much responsibility on for my future and destiny had finally come: Sunday, March 17, 2024, the morning of the Los Angeles Marathon on St. Patrick's Day. I had consumed water, coffee, 1.5 protein bars, Naproxen (generic Aleve), and a caffeinated Celsius energy drink. It was just after 5:00 a.m., and we were out on the quiet and empty streets of LA walking to our shuttle. It was beautiful and so peaceful, the buildings, tall, shiny, and pristine. They seemed so grand and important next to me, and I just wanted to be still and bask in their magnificence, but there was no time for that, especially once we caught up to some other runners and realized the shuttle pickup was in the opposite direction. We reversed and went... that... way.

We finally made to the shuttle, so we could hurry up and wait. The very long lines included all types of runners, such as high school teams that all needed to be transported together. I was told that five shuttles were running from our pick-up point, but based on elapsed time, that did not seem to be the case. Due to the wind – it was not windy; and I have run in the face of wind, my nemesis – everyone on the shuttle had to be seated on as opposed to riders being able to stand on the shuttle and hold onto the poles. This was yet again another obstacle, more spiritual warfare. We met another solo runner, Suzanne, from Northern California, and the three of us decided to catch an Uber together.

Unfortunately, our Uber driver seemed unaware of the LA Marathon. The street closures were already in effect, and he literally drove us to roadblock after roadblock. He seemed completely baffled. David brought up a driving street map provided by the LA Marathon folks. I convinced our driver to please take the freeway, and we were able to direct him to the exits and drop off area, only to arrive minutes before the 7:00 a.m. race start time.

Since I was only going to cross the start line, I figured,

why not check out the Start Line Hospitality tent as I now had to use the restroom and the other restrooms still had lines? The tent was basically empty, so I was in and out. I made a quick cup of coffee for David and grabbed two bananas and a fruit cup for him because he loves fruit, and I tried to stuff down my shame at having paid $150 for this experience.

CHAPTER 4:

MY RACE

By the time I crossed the start line at 7:28 a.m., it already looked like the ghost of a marathon. A party marked by a kaleidoscope of discarded goo energy gel packets, shiny metallic blankets, and sweatshirts by the thousands... the sacrificial charity donation of so many runners.

"And we still have people crossing the start line," the announcer's voice boomed over the loud speaker. That was me, *people*, along with a fair number of other runners.

Jesus said, if we only had the faith of a tiny mustard seed, we could move mountains. Something happened to me when I crossed that start line. I believe the Holy Spirit descended upon me. My right knee pain seemed so mild. I was overcome with pure joy and delight. Twelve minutes later, at 7:40 a.m., I texted David, "I'm not sure what's happening. I cannot run or jog, but I am walking, and I feel inspired to keep walking further." Then, again at 8:02 a.m., I texted, "Hi, I think you should go back to the hotel and pack up the room because there's a fire in me right now. I want to walk and finish this race."

The LA Marathon keeps the streets closed for six hours and 30 minutes until the last person has crossed the start line. That means that the race should be finished with a 15-minute per mile average pace or faster. After that, participants can still finish the race, but they need to move to the sidewalk. I thought, maybe I could do the 15-minute per mile pace, but according to my Garmin watch, my fastest mile was a slow 16:54.

So, for me, it was unlike any race I had been in before. Because I had started so late, and I was walking, it was like I was in the discarded dust of the LA Marathon. I would come to a water station, and all I would see was what was left behind: hundreds, likely thousands, of water cups spread out on the edges of the street. There was usually a volunteer who could get me water, though, if I asked.

At times, I felt like I was being chased by one of the many big yellow street sweeping trucks or moving trucks, packing up the tables and water stations, just as I was arriving. I was walking on the edge of a race that was nipping at my heels, closing down before my very eyes, the shadow of the LA Marathon.

To me, it was pure joy. I wanted to pinch myself. I could not believe it. My running book and program, *The Non-Runner's Marathon Trainer,* advised that there was no shame in walking. Now, they were not necessarily referring to *walking* the *entire* marathon because I think a reasonable person – and most certainly a runner – would consider it borderline insanity. I have read that the experienced marathoner would prefer a DNF (Did Not Finished) as opposed to walking a marathon. But I had too much riding on this race… my divine destiny, for starters. In *The Non-Runner's Marathon Trainer,* I learned that a runner may have to walk from time to time, and if that time ever came, then one was to walk tall, confident, and with their head held high. That is exactly what I did. Early in the race, I saw two fit men around my age who were walking, one wearing the oh-so-familiar mask of pain on his face. "Are you guys injured?" I asked. They laughed, and one of them replied, "We're always injured." I could relate.

In those moments, I was not focused on my limitations. I was walking in a miracle. I would text updates to David. "Mile 4! God is good!" at 8:37 a.m. "10K check [6.2 miles]" at 9:15 a.m., to which he responded, "You go girl. Champion." Champion, the word that was threaded throughout my motivational speech songs. A champion does not quit, does not give up, stays in the game, does not argue for their limitations. That was me; it was who I aspired to be. "Mile 10," I texted at 10:25 a.m.

As with all epic adventures, there were some challenges. It started to get hot. Multiple times, I thanked God that I wore a bright pink T-back runner's tank top under my Shamrock green fleece sweatshirt. I had first put on a long sleeve shirt in the hotel room, and I thankfully felt too warm that I swapped it for the tank top that I was now wearing. I had applied sunblock in multiple layers and high strength to my face, and I was wearing a water wicking baseball cap. I had some SPF on my neck, chest, and shoulders, but nothing on my arms or back. I tied my sweatshirt over my shoulders to protect my skin from getting sun burned.

I was on a mission to finish the LA Marathon and similarly on a mission to get sunblock. The problem was that because I was so slow and so far behind, the would-be aid stations were no longer visible or open by the time that I reached them. "Reached them" is even a stretch of the imagination, because they were non-existent. What I did see were red medical vehicles, what I can best describe as a golf cart version of a stretch limo. I spoke to the workers in a few of these vehicles, and they did not have sunscreen or ibuprofen. These vehicles, as I understood, were to pick up folks who were injured or who needed to stop their marathon. When I asked one of these medical workers about sunscreen, he offered to drive me to the next aid station. I tried not to show my offense at his kindness. The audacity! I was going to walk *every* step. And so, I faced the natural consequences of my determination, arriving at the would-be aid stations only to find a non-existent mirage.

The Lord provides, so I did find what I needed in different ways. I had taken Naproxen that morning (generic Aleve), which is what I had been taking for my injury and even for my long training runs. I was doing surprisingly well, all things considered, but I wanted to prevent my pain from escalating. At 10:36 a.m. I texted David that a nice lady gave me two Advil. This lady, as I learned, was one of several people rotating in and out of the race to walk with Legacy Bob, a man who had been participating in the LA marathon since it first began 39 years ago. While I would never advocate taking medication from a stranger, I figured that the companion of an esteemed legacy runner, was the type of person that I could trust to give me two Advil.

Throughout the race course, different individuals and organizations were set up on the sidelines performing with instruments, giving out water, energy drinks, sugary treats, and more. I walked up to one such table hopeful to save my skin from burning.

"Do you have any sunblock?" I asked the volunteer.

"No," she said, with disappointment on her face. Then she suddenly lit up. "You know what, I think I have some sunscreen in my purse."

Low and behold, she dug into her personal handbag and pulled out an individual packet of Banana Boat SPF 30. It was so humbling to see her heart for service and desire to go above and beyond to help me.

I tore into the packet as I continued on my journey and slathered sunblock on my arms, neck, and exposed back areas. Then, I tied my Shamrock green sweatshirt around my waist and kept moving forward. I thought about letting my sweatshirt go, just like all of the discarded sweatshirts I saw at the start line, but my friend Tonia had given it to me more than 20 years ago, and I was not ready to release it in that moment. The sweatshirt would stay with me through to the finish line. It all worked because I did not burn at all. Praise God!

During long runs, many runners consume "goo" as a food/energy source. I had never tried goo because I have a sensitive stomach, and the sugar content tended to be higher than what I normally eat. During training, I would bring one, possibly two, protein bars with me – containing carbohydrates, but a low sugar content – that I would eat on my runs. The morning of the LA Marathon, just as we were standing outside of the hotel elevator, I realized I had forgotten to put protein bars in my runner's pack. David offered to go back and get them, but I thought it was no big deal since my intention was to cross the start line and go home. This was a decision I would come to regret. My faith was so small;

I do not know why I ever doubted God for one second.

To my surprise, much like the aid stations, food was not plentiful on the marathon course. It may have been, but again, I was in the ghost of the marathon, the marathon dust, where everything was shutting down behind me. I had consumed about 300 calories that morning, and I knew I needed more fuel. Then, I came upon a mirage that did not fade away, a woman standing with Ziplock bags full of cold orange slices and tangerines, pulled fresh from her icy cooler. I graciously accepted one of these precious bags like it was gold. I do not remember a time when oranges have ever tasted so delicious. They paired well with my orange flavored zero sugar electrolyte water that David had filled for me in my runner's belt water bottles before we left our hotel room.

With the sunscreen, Advil, and nourishment, I think I perked up a little bit and appeared more approachable. I was walking alongside a husband and wife, who were around 10 years older than me. I noticed them keeping pace with me.

"So, what are you walking for? Any special cause?" the wife kindly asked me.

Uh, to meet my goal of finishing a marathon, to cross the finish line and have the Holy Spirit descend upon me with my divine destiny and a new name, I thought to myself.

Instead, I opted to go with, "Oh, I trained for the marathon.

I had an injury, but I still wanted to come out here today, if I could. So, I'm basically just here to finish the marathon."

"We're in from Boston, here on vacation," the husband explained.

That's when I realized, they did not have bibs on. They told me about how they were on foot, sightseeing, and how they were accidentally walking the course of the LA Marathon. To me that was super cool, the type of stuff my runner's heart loved to geek out about, stumbling upon a marathon.

We chatted for a few minutes, and then they politely made their exit from the marathon course (aka, the open street) to the sidewalk. Nevertheless, my heart was warmed to speak to people who had traveled across the country for the same site seeing that I was so intimately privy to via the amazing LA Marathon course, where all streets closed down for race participants like me. I reminded myself how blessed I was to be part of this amazing experience.

David continued to track my phone and was therefore able to follow me through the race course so he could be sure to meet me at the finish line. At 10:37 he texted, "I'm very proud of you. Looks like you're approaching Hollywood and Vine. I texted back at 11:24 a.m. "Half marathon mark. It took me just under four hours, so God willing I can do this whole thing around 3:20 p.m."

I felt on fire at that point. I had walked 13.1 miles. In

training, I had run – not walked – six runs in excess of a half marathon. I could do this. At mile 13, my pace was 19:25. I literally picked up the pace a little, finishing mile 14 at 19:05, mile 15 at 17:50, and mile 16 at 17:54. I would later come to regret pushing myself, but it was in this time frame that I reached Beverly Hills and Rodeo Drive at mile 17. I was blinded by the bling, so to speak. I was not just doing something hard. In that moment, I was overcome by how glamourous it all seemed, walking down Rodeo Drive, the street completely open. Me, feeling so confident, and like I had a right to be there, as opposed to feeling intimidated by the expensive designer shops that were not really in my league or lifestyle. I felt like I belonged in this place, and I was caught up in a worldly mindset that made me feel invincible, before I would slowly begin to crash.

◆ ◆ ◆

My ghost of a marathon transformed, just after the mile 18 marker, when I was suddenly in the thick of the action and could pan my eyes to see hundreds, perhaps thousands of people. I had arrived at the finish line, so to speak. For the entire race, I had walked an unrepeated path, so every mile brought new sights, new sounds, new landmarks to see and experience. I was now entering the part of the race that would loop from about mile 18 to mile 22 and then circle back to the finish line at mile

26.2. I was on one side of the street, and the other side was crowded with runners, approaching the finish line. The sidelines were overflowing with volunteers and fans cheering on their loved ones. It was exciting because, in a way, I had finally caught up to the marathon. Instead of it closing down behind me, it was hooting and hollering, in epic and amazing ways for all of those finishers.

I could see the finish line, but in my mind, it seemed further and further away. During training, my longest runs were 18 miles. I ran them, not walked. Some programs push runners up to 20 miles, but I was well within the range of a typical training program. Plus, I followed a research-based program. Passing 18 miles, even though I was not running, meant that I was going further than I had ever gone before. So, I was caught up in my head, but mostly I was caught up in my body that was screaming PAIN. Loudly. Clearly.

David must have somehow sensed this through our strong connection and bond. At 12:51 p.m. he texted me, with our pet name for each other, "Hi cat. Hope you're ok." I responded back right away, "Yeah, I think I'm at the point where [I need] more pain medicine, but I'm sticking it out. I'll be at mile 18 soon." He responded back, encouraging me, "Love you, proud of you, keep going."

Fortunately for me, because I had finally caught up to the

marathon, I had also caught up to the resources, which were open and available. I graciously accepted a peanut butter granola bar from a volunteer. It was a treasure. My calorie intake for the day was low. I had consumed 1.5 protein bars, some orange slices, a tangerine, two small pretzels, water, xero calorie electrolyte drink, and now a granola bar. I also had access to the medical aid station. I was handed a clipboard where I scribbled my name and bib number, and traded the clipboard back for two more Advil.

The two Advil were very much needed because I realized that both of my feet were blistered. I could not see the blisters beneath my ankle sleeves, $20 runner socks, and Saucony running shoes, but they made their presence known. I was no stranger to blisters. During one of my long Saturday morning training runs, I came home to find a blister on the interior side of my right big toe. I do not exaggerate when I say that the blister was like a sixth toe, *larger* in fact than my baby toe. I could not risk popping it and running with raw skin, so I learned to slather it with Aquaphor, take advantage of its cycle of slowly draining and refilling, and to adjust it and layer it slightly above my second toe. A lot of ick factor was involved as I nurtured my enormous blister. Now, as I was in the marathon with new blisters, plural, on both of my feet, I felt a sense of comradery and normalcy. I thought of the LA Marathon program I received at the Lifestyle Expo Fair, which had the most beautiful message to participants along with this to say about blisters, "You nursed your blisters and ran through the pain." I thought of Cheryl Strayed's memoir *Wild*, one of my favorite reads of 2023. Strayed tells her story of the many weeks she spent walking the Pacific Crest Trail, in all kinds of weather, in rugged nature, with painful blisters on her feet, and at one point losing a boot and having to walk in shower sandals to the next rest stop. My blisters had nothing on what this hero had experienced. Just thinking about Strayed inspired and encouraged me, and I walked on.

Not everyone felt as encouraged. Somewhere between mile 18 and mile 19, another walker edged up to me, frustrated, exasperation fuming off of his 30-something-year-old face.

"I just saw someone fully cut across and cheat," he said looking to commiserate an injustice he had just witnessed.

My eyes followed where he was pointing, but it was impossible to discern who he was referring to as my gaze spanned hundreds of runners who were nearing the finish line. We were on one side of the road, and they were on the other, separated by a grassy median strip filled with lawn chairs, pop up tents, fans, food, and more. We were less than 50 feet away from the other side of the street, where we could look back and see the finish line. While the finish line may have looked close, for us, it was about another eight miles away.

"I mean, why cheat like that? This is something you do for

yourself," the young man said.

I wondered at his story, cognizant that every runner was here for a reason. Was he in pain, walking with a fracture like me? There was some reason he was walking and not running. Some reason why he was here. I wish I had asked. Instead, I just said what I thought he wanted to hear.

"Right, I mean the race has already been won at this point," I agreed. "It's about the personal achievement."

"It's just not right," he shook his head.

I wanted to lift his spirits and make him feel better about the whole thing. "Don't worry. The race tracks us along the way. Remember how we had to walk over that thing, like at the start line, that recorded us at different marks like 5K and 20K?"

He nodded slowly, though not looking thoroughly convinced.

"Her data won't add up. They will catch her on the back end of things and know that she cheated," I assured him.

"Yeah, well, I don't know."

I didn't know either. At the end of the day, who would know? I knew I would feel cheated if I had gone this far to not to have my Garmin watch document that I had *completed* the 26.2-mile marathon. Ultimately, I would know, and that would be enough. And so, I continued to walk on.

Through most of my marathon, the mile markers had been

taken down by the time I reached them. When I caught up with the race, however, I got to see all of the large vertical banner size mile markers (perhaps 15 to 20 ft. tall) that both encouraged and taunted me because I had come so far, yet I had so much further to go. It was around 1:38 p.m. at this point because I texted David, "I just hit mile 20. I did get some more Advil. I did get a granola bar. It seems a little impossible to know that I'm gonna walk for two more hours, so please pray for [me] hard." He responded, "You've got this, pie." Pie was our most favorite nickname for each other (next to Cat). "We serve the God of impossibilities. I love you, and you got this. Praying for you. Love you."

At 2:12 p.m. David texted, "I am at the finish line. You are a Champion." I responded back right away, "I am slowing down because the pain is so great, so it could be maybe an hour and a half before I cross the finish line." Then about 10 minutes later at 2:24 p.m. I wrote, "I just hit mile 22. It took me like 23 or 24 minutes to complete that mile." "Praying" with a folded hands emoji was David's response to me.

At 2:36 p.m. he wrote, "We can't get to the runners. So, you will need to cross the finish line and then head right down to Constellation Street. You will see the runners going that way. Cell service is very spotty." I was coming close to the end of myself. I was grumpy to say the least, so I responded, "Pie, please don't stress me out with this stuff right now. It's gonna be another hour for me. I'm fighting, back tears." He sent me another folded hands emoji and a heart to which I replied, "If you could take texting you off of my plate right now, that would be great."

◆ ◆ ◆

Throughout the race, I had thought of Dean Karnazes. I became a fan of his when I read *Ultra Marathon Man*, a memoir that details his adventures running 100-mile races, solo relay races, a marathon in Antarctica, and so many other feats that absolutely blew my mind. I remembered a video I watched where Karnazes was talking about how sometimes during a race he would run for hours just thinking "next step, next step" over and over again. Be. Like. Dean. I was experiencing my miracle marathon while feeling like I was in the pit of hell. The irony was not lost on me. And so, again, and again, I tried the Karnazes mantra, "next step, next step, next step." It seemed like a fitting message because I could literally feel every... single... step.

I had simultaneously entered into a marathon cry session. I am not a fan of crying in public, displaying so much weakness and vulnerability. My dad may have been dead, but – *Damnit girl! You can't cry every time something doesn't go your way!* – certainly lived on in my mind. True to form, I did my best to mask my emotions by crying silently. Tears trickled down my face without any audible sobs, and I did not dare touch my cheeks to wipe them away. Let them pour down like sweat. The temperature was somewhere in the 70's by now; I felt hot in the direct sunlight, yet I was not moving fast enough to even be breaking a sweat. All I had were my tears.

And my pain. It was certainly physical. My right knee, left knee, both shins, my feet, my back. It all just ached and ached and felt so very sore. Of course, I also felt mental anguish. I was in the middle of this miracle, and I would accomplish my stated goal, which was to finish the race, but all of the glory was stripped away. I was just walking a marathon, and not speed walking, not even at a decent cadence, just the pace of next step, next step. Looking back now, it was all for God's glory. If I had run, finished at a decent pace, I know myself, and I would have been boasting about my metrics. It was not until many days after the race had ended that I would have my 2 Timothy 4:7-8 moment, "I have fought the good fight, I have finished the race, I have kept the faith. Now there is in store for me the crown of righteousness, which the Lord, the righteous Judge, will award me on that day – and not only to me, but to all who longed for His appearing."

God did appear for me, and he showed up for me, in ways I could not have imagined because I had the faith to simply cross the start line. In that moment though, in my pain, while experiencing my miracle, I was feeling sorry for myself. I was certainly caught up in the flesh, my flesh. My motivational speech songs had prepped me with phrases like "don't back down from the pain; feel no pain" or "a champion's workout begins when pain arrives." In a way, this backfired because I had listened over and over and over again about how I was supposed to be immune to the pain. And clearly, I was not.

I thought about Jesus on the road to Calvary. I thought of His pain, and suffering, His willingness to give his life for all of humanity, to bear the weight of the world. I even felt a little shameful, because comparing my race to what Jesus did on the cross was a wild stretch of the imagination. It was delusional, blasphemy perhaps. How dare I! Who was I? And yet, who was I not? I was a child of God, of the most high king. I took some comfort in knowing that like Jesus, I was walking a long way in pain, and in that, I could share in the suffering of Christ. "For the more we suffer for Christ, the more God will shower us with His comfort through Christ," 2 Cor 1:5.

My pain was obvious to everyone who passed me by. I was about two miles shy of the finish line when another legacy runner approached me.

"You think you gonna make it?" he asked.

Inwardly, I took offence at his kindness. Of course, I was going to make it! I did not come this far to quit with only two miles left! I imagined crazy scenarios – crawling, rolling, dragging my body with my arms propelling me forward to the finish line – all which would have ironically been far more painful than walking slowly, with caution, as I was. No matter what, I would make it across that finish line.

"Yes," I meekly replied. "I'm going to finish."

"Here," he said pressing a coin into my hand. "It's a souvenir for you."

It was a penny that had been painted with what looked like turquoise glitter nail polish on one side and light green nail polish on the other side, with "LA 26.2" written in black sharpie. It was kind of cool. A souvenir from a real legacy runner who was distinguished with his special shirt, with his name and the names of his entire cohort on it. I pictured his granddaughter or other family members prepping all kinds of pennies for him to give away to people like me as they cheered him on with love. I'm sure there was a story behind why he gave out pennies, and now, this penny was a part of my story.

◆ ◆ ◆

In these last few miles, the race that had been shutting down all around me, that I finally caught up to, was officially shutting down. This time, for real. The roads were going to open back up to regular street traffic. It sounded terrifying. This alone was enough to encourage me to walk as fast as I possibly could. All of us runners – aka walkers – were kindly asked to move to the sidewalk. Volunteers – in their designated shirts – were cruising by on bicycles, tallying how many participants were left, how many stragglers.

It reminded me of what I used to do as an elementary school principal. I would be out in the parking lot at dismissal time, and about 20 minutes or so after school had ended, I would round up all of the children who still had not been picked up and take them up to the safety of the office where they could be supervised and have someone in their family called to pick them up. Sometimes, students would try to hide outside because they were embarrassed, simply did not want to go to the office, or they knew their parent would be upset with them, inconvenienced that now they had to come to the office to sign out their child as opposed to a quick pick up in the parking lot. I felt like one of those kids.

I had to keep moving so that the volunteers would not send someone to pick me up. At 3:48 p.m. I resumed texting and updated David, "I'm about a mile away." Then, somewhere in that last mile, David just magically appeared, waiting for me along the homestretch. Tall, suntanned, and handsome, with his perfect head of full, enviable hair. There was my guy, whom I had met when I was 18-years-old, in the breakroom of an office where I was working as a temp. It was love at first sight. Over the years, I would feel it again and again, at times when I saw my husband unexpectedly... in that fraction of a second before I recognized who he was, I would feel it all over again, that feeling of love at first sight, the fluttering in my stomach and heart. My husband and my forever love.

He had my white sweatshirt draped over his shoulders. Thoughtful. On long runs, I would come home soaked, drenched in head to toe sweat. I wouldn't really notice as I ran, but after I stopped, it did not take long until I began to feel cold under the cling of my wet attire. David was probably thinking of this as he brought a fresh sweatshirt for me to wear. Except, I really was not sweating.

And when I saw him, my silent tears, turned to messy, gasping sobs. He enveloped me in his arms.

"What are you doing here?" I asked. Meaning here. On the race course. Not at the finish line.

"I wasn't sure I was going to be able to do it, but they opened things up a bit, and I thought I would finish the race with you."

His brown eyes were sparkling at me and his head was shaking back and forth in disbelief. "You are amazing. I can't believe you did it."

David called me amazing. It was enough for me to lose it. He was my safe place and refuge. A natural – a normal – thought might be with my loving husband by my side, I could do anything. Instead, I told David, I could not walk side by side with him because it made me too emotional, too comforted. Looking back, I sometimes wonder why I cannot be more easygoing and agreeable. There are so many times when I could have done "hard" better instead of making "hard" even harder on myself. But I was willing to do hard things, and for this I was grateful. I tried to give myself grace and take my good qualities with my not-so-good qualities.

David walked behind me, and let me do my thing. He was so kind, not offended, not hurt. Little did I know it at the time, but he had spent two hours driving what should have taken 10 minutes to get from our hotel to the race parking lot. Two hours. His own marathon of a day! But I would hear none of that until much later. In that moment, he was there just for me.

As I saw various walkers like me, in pain, determined to finish their marathon, I was struck by the kindness of others that I had witnessed over and over that day and even now at the very end. Everyone who was still in the race was walking, and it seemed to me that many were suffering. A lady off to the side had a huge spray bottle filled with some sort of topical pain relief, and she was misting down anyone who accepted her offer. She was jovial, desiring to help and give of herself. I had leggings on, so I figured whatever was in the spray bottle would not work over my clothing, but I still caught a bit of her joy. I saw another participant who was obviously limping in what looked to be an injury that had occurred during the race. Next to her was a volunteer speaking life into her, telling her she would not leave her side, asking her if she could do it, telling her that the finish line was up ahead; we could see it in the distance.

And what was I seeing? As I approached the finish line, I realized that even that, too, was coming down. The finish line banner was half pealed down from what looked to be a large freeway sign, or perhaps an onramp.

"Where's the finish line?" I looked back and asked David in a panic.

"It's just up ahead to the right," David assured me.

The finish line had been rerouted. I should have expected this. The race directions were clear. The race started at 7:00 a.m. The roads would stay closed for six and a half hours after the last runner had crossed the start line, which was a very generous 15-minute per mile pace. I had crossed the start line at 7:28 a.m., so even if the last person crossed the start line an hour after the race began, at 8:00 a.m. – which I doubted was likely – that would put the end time at 2:30 p.m. It was now after 4:00 p.m., and I was clearly aware that the roads had opened back up to street traffic. I thought it was incredibly charitable – almost lavish – that the folks in charge of the LA Marathon, still allowed people to finish the race, even after six hours and 30 minutes. Nevertheless, I was a bit heartbroken that I would not get to cross the big grand finish line, and I would instead have to cross the alternate and much smaller rerouted finish line, minus the grandiose fanfare. Really, what did I expect? I would later come to understand, that even the alternate finish line was for my growth and ultimately for God's glory. It was another way for me to peel away at myself and to release my ego and my pride so that I was fully reliant on Him. So that I could truly say, "To God be the glory."

"The finish line is just up ahead, Pie, to the right of the bleachers," David said. The silver metallic stadium style bleachers must have been brought in for the race. If David had not told me – and volunteers with air filled neon pointers had not been directing the way – I could have very well missed the finish line. It was simply a small light blue banner, swaying upward toward the sky, with FINISH displayed in all white caps.

This was the moment. Half smiling, silently crying, trying to hide my mask of pain, I walked up to the finish line. David was behind me and then ahead of me snapping pictures with his iPhone. At 4:22 p.m., I crossed the finish line. It took me eight hours, 54 minutes and 59 seconds to finish the LA Marathon. My average pace was 20 minute and 24 second miles. In my gender and age category (women aged 40-44), I finished in 823rd place of 830.

When I crossed that finish line, I felt more defeat than victory. It was not a road to Damascus moment. I did not see bright lights, hear the voice of God, have a vision or prophetic word, or suddenly know my new name. It all felt anticlimactic. It was just like God, though, to do the opposite of what I might have expected. I thought my miracle would come at the finish line, and He brought it to me at the start line. I did not go from limping around my hotel room with a fractured knee the night before to walking an entire marathon the very next day without a miracle. This much I knew.

CHAPTER 5:
AFTER THE MARATHON

Just like every other participant, I was handed a finisher medal and offered carb-filled snacks and electrolyte water which I declined because I knew David would have what I wanted in the car.

The car!

"Pie, where is the car?" I whine-cried.

"It's up ahead about half a mile from here."

Half a mile? Half a mile! I saw a shaded patch of thick green grass to my right, and all I wanted to do was lie down in it and sleep until the next morning. I did not think I could walk another half of a mile.

What I had learned from participating in races is that it is easy for runners – or in my case walkers – to exceed and surpass the distance of the precisely measured race course. Even though the marathon was 26.2 miles, as standard, my Garmin watch had me at 26.62 miles when I crossed the finish line. I had already gone close to an extra half mile. This typically occurs through bobbing and weaving past other runners, something I did not do. For me, it might have just been not walking perfectly straight across the wide road, or little extra stops I made to the aid station, stops made looking for aid stations, the one stop about halfway through the race to use the porta-potty, so little things like that. All of those extra steps added up. And now, David was asking me to go an extra half mile, putting my entire distance in excess of 27 miles. Not to mention, I walked before the race to get to the shuttle, to the start line, and so on. It was silly; I had already gone this far. What was another half mile? In my mind, though, it seemed impossible.

"Are we there yet? How much further?" I repeatedly asked David over and over again, like a nagging child.

He kept encouraging me, telling me how "amazing" I was, and it was not just lip service, either. He truly believed it. He was blown away that I had finished the race. David knew it was through the power of God, but he also knew my humanity more than anyone. He had been through a fracture with me before and saw firsthand that what I had experienced was truly a miracle.

We finally made it to the car, and I was so grateful to sit down and rest. David had our stash of protein bars, caffeinated Celsius energy drinks, and naproxen pain medication, all of which I eagerly consumed. David mapped our course back home and started driving, and in about 10 minutes, I started to feel better. My stress was relieved as was my tearful and pitiful disposition. Before I knew it, I was on my phone, placing our dinner order for some carbohydrate rich fish tacos, beans, and rice (cauliflower rice for me as I was not completely forgone from my ways).

My mom and our three dogs were waiting for us at home in Anaheim. As we sat at our dining room table, savoring our meal, I confessed everything to my mom: my injury, my faith, my miracle. She was not surprised, not phased at all.

"Somehow I just knew it," she said. "I knew you were injured. And I just prayed to God, 'please let her finish the race,' because I knew that was all you wanted, to finish the race," she said, in almost a whisper, holding back the tears that glistened her eyes.

My mom was not the only person who had a supernatural knowledge about me. My best friend Ramina – the one who had burnt a candle for me and placed it next to the rock my dad had given her two decades ago – also had an experience where she was overcome with emotion for me. Like my mom, she knew nothing of my injury or my hope for a miracle. It would be a month later when I would confess everything to Ramina.

The day of the LA Marathon, Ramina and her family were heading out for a spring break trip to Solvang. Originally, I was planning to join her for spring break, until my training runs exceeded the three-hour mark, and it took me the remainder of every Saturday to recover. I realized that my body would not be physically ready to go on vacation immediately following the LA Marathon, and Ramina understood. Interestingly enough, as she and her family were driving out to Solvang, Ramina could see the LA Marathon happening from the freeway. The way she explained it, she burst into tears crying for me.

"What is wrong with you?" her husband had asked her.

"I don't know, I just feel so emotional for Helene," she told him as she thought of me out there finishing my race. Ramina did not know that I only showed up to cross the start line and that a miracle would happen for me. Something in her heart felt me and God's presence over me.

"I love you deep, Lene," she often says to me. Deep. There was something supernatural about the love of both a true friend and a mother. I could not hide my real self from either of them, because love was written on their hearts, and this love revealed the truth.

In the days that followed the LA Marathon, I experienced

a surprising amount of pain all over my body. The pain scared me because I worried that I had further injured myself. In reality, it turns out that walking over 27 miles, puts a strain on the body. The entire body. My back, my legs, my shins, my knees. So many parts ached and ached. I expected that I would need time to recover, but I did not expect the pain to feel so intense and unrelenting.

I remembered that I had a TENS (Transcutaneous Electrical Nerve Stimulation) machine that someone had given us years ago that we had never used. It looked like a cell phone, and after watching a few videos online, I could see that it was easy to use. I plugged in the electrodes and placed the small pads on my legs, feet, back, and so on, letting the waves of electrical impulses sooth my body. Over the next few days, the TENS machine became my best friend, that, along with the regular icing of my shins and knees. My mom stayed on to visit, and since she had a torn meniscus – what a pair we were! – she was happy to have low key days with me during my spring break. I was so very grateful for this time off from work. After about three or four days, my body aches subsided, and all that remained was the pain in my right knee and shin area, at the same pain level that it was at before the marathon.

I mostly followed the doctor's orders, from when I went to see the orthopedic surgeon before the marathon. I say mostly followed. First of all, I was not supposed to even attempt to walk the marathon. My doctor said in addition to risking further injury from overuse, I could get pushed or fall down. God was so good. In the ghost of the marathon that I walked, no one was close enough or fast enough to speed past me.

I did follow doctor's orders because I stopped all running. Not because I wanted to, but because it was too painful. David and I resumed our morning weightlifting workouts. I modified some of the leg exercises, but I got myself to a point where I could deadlift over 100 pounds. I was still a novice, but that would be an example of not following doctor's orders.

It astonishes me how long one has to wait to get an MRI. For me, it would be almost two months on May 8, 2024. The MRI revealed the reappearance of a stress fracture – or overuse fracture from too much running – of my proximal tibia. The MRI also showed "mild edema in the infrapatellar fat pad, suggestive of a patellar tendon-lateral femoral condyle correction syndrome". This meant that there was swelling in the fat pad below my knee cap. This was due to the patellar tendon – which connects my kneecap (patella) to my shinbone – rubbing against the lateral femoral condyle (the bone at the end of my thigh bone); this condition can result in pain and inflammation around the kneecap. Womp, womp.

In a strange way, I found my MRI report exciting because I

had a medically verifiable miracle. It wasn't just that my doctor thought I had a fracture – the MRI proved it. I knew what God had done for me; I did not need a test result to prove how God had interceded for me at the LA Marathon. But I also knew that I wanted to tell my story to a world where we humans have a tendency to default to a Doubting Thomas mentality. The MRI alleviated those doubts. It would be almost four months after my injury until I would jog again, about two miles on flat park terrain at a slow 12:13 minute per mile average pace.

And then what of my new name? On June 6, 2024, I was driving to work, and my new name came to me instantly and confidently: Gloria.

"What, am I supposed to call you Gloria now?" David asked when I texted him with excitement.

No. I wasn't really sure what to do. I would leave it to God to reveal the what and how of this new name. And I start with this, the byline for my marathon miracle story, by Helene "Gloria" Morris.

Final Thoughts

And I close with this… remember, you can be in the middle of a miracle right now and not even know it. It might not look like anything you ever expected. God will most definitely surprise you. In doing so, you may surprise yourself. Like me, you could break the generational bondage of lies that have been spoken over your life. While these lies may have been in an effort to protect you, they could have caused a lifetime of self-limiting beliefs, like thinking you could never run when in reality, you were born to run. Or maybe, like me, you think you should never let anyone see you cry, so you try to hold all of your emotions inside. Only later do you realize that the person who told you not to cry, never let anyone see him cry. I went my whole life and *never* saw my dad cry… maybe if he had cried, those tears would have helped him to live.

The moral of this story is to have the faith – like a mustard seed – to show up and cross the start line. Because you have to start to start. Let that sink in: you have to start to start. And if you do that, God will come through for you. He will bring you to the finish line. He will give you a testimony… and it will be for HIS glory, and in this case, for his Gloria.

REFERENCES AND INSPIRATION

References and Inspriation

Alsbrooks, B. (n.d.). Motivational speech songs [Music]. Apple Music. https://music.apple.com

Burke Harris, N. (2018). *The deepest well: Healing the long-term effects of childhood adversity.* Houghton Mifflin Harcourt.

Carr, A. (2015). *Quit drinking without willpower: Be a happy nondrinker.* Allen Carr'sEasyway.

Day, A. (2015). "Rise up" [Song]. On *Cheers to the Fall*. Warner Records.

Delaware Physical Therapy Clinic. (n.d.). *Treadmill running program.* University of Delaware. https://cpb-us-w2.wpmucdn.com/sites.udel.edu/dist/c/3448/files/2016/10/running_progression_2015-orf1zr.pdf

Douglas, S. (2018). *Running is my therapy: Relieve stress and anxiety, fight depression, ditch bad habits, and live happier.* The Experiment.

Elrod, H. (2017). *The miracle morning: The six habits that will transform your life before 8AM.* John Murray Learning

Fearless Motivation. (n.d.). Motivational speech songs [Music].

Apple Music. https://music.apple.com

Karnazes, D. (2006). *Ultramarathon man: Confessions of an all-night runner*. TarcherPerigee.

Kirtley, D. (n.d.). *@fiftyfitnessjourney* [Instagram profile]. Instagram. Retrieved August 12, 2023, from https://www.instagram.com/fiftyfitnessjourney

Matthews, M. (2019). *Thinner leaner stronger: The simple science of building the ultimate female body (3rd ed.).* Waterbury Publications.

McDougall, C. (2009). *Born to run: A hidden tribe, superathletes, and the greatest race the world has never seen.* Knopf.

Ruiz, D. M. (1997). *The four agreements: A practical guide to personal freedom.* Amber-Allen Publishing.

Strayed, C. (2012). *Wild: From lost to found on the Pacific Crest Trail.* Knopf.

The Bible. (n.d.). *Holy Bible.* Various Publishers.

Whitsett, D. A., Dolgener, F. A., & Kole, T. M. (1998). *The non-runner's marathon trainer.* McGraw-Hill Education.

2024 LA Marathon Race Program. (2024). *2024 LA Marathon race program.*

ABOUT THE AUTHOR

Helene "Gloria" Morris

Helene "Gloria" Morris has served as an educator for over 20 years. She holds a Bachelor of Arts in Communications Public Relations from California State University Fullerton, two teaching credentials from San Diego State University, a Master of Science in Education Administration from Pepperdine University, and a Doctorate of Education from USC. Helene is passionate about exercise, nutrition, mental health, and a personal calling to end suicide. Helene is grounded by her deep faith, family, core values, and commitment to rise before dawn each day and fulfill the divine purposes for her life. Helene lives in Anaheim with her husband, David, and their three dogs.

Printed in Great Britain
by Amazon